Animal watch

Written by
ROGER FEW
Consultant
DR PHIL WHITFIELD

A Dorling Kindersley Book

Dorling **DK** Kindersley

LONDON, NEW YORK, SYDNEY, DELHI,
PARIS, MUNICH, and JOHANNESBURG

Senior Art Editor Marcus James
Senior Editor Fran Jones
Managing Editor Sue Grabham
Senior Managing Art Editor Julia Harris
Picture Researchers Michele Faram and Amanda Russell
Production Nicola Torode and Jenny Jacoby
DTP Designer Nomazwe Madonko
US Editor Margaret Parrish

Designed and edited by Bookwork
Art Editor Jill Plank **Editor** Louise Pritchard
Assistant Art Editor Yolanda Belton
Assistant Editor Annabel Blackledge

First American edition 2001
00 01 02 03 04 05 10 9 8 7 6 5 4 3 2 1

Published in the United States by
Dorling Kindersley Publishing Inc.
95 Madison Avenue
New York, New York 10016

The CIP record for this book is available
from the Library of Congress

ISBN 0-7894-7766-1

Reproduced by Colourscan, Singapore
Printed and bound in China by L. Rex Printing Co., Ltd.

See our complete catalog at
www.dk.com

Contents

Introduction

We share our planet

with a huge variety of wildlife. Across the globe, on land and in the oceans, there are animals of all shapes and sizes – creatures that crawl, slide, run, swim, fly, or burrow. Each type of animal is called a species, and the more we learn about the Earth, the more species we realize are living alongside us. Scientists have already discovered about 1.7 million species, and every year they find about 13,000 new ones. It is unlikely that there are many unknown large animals, such as mammals and birds, but there could still be millions of small creatures, such as insects, spiders, shellfish, and worms, waiting to be discovered.

As animals go through their lives, eating, breeding, traveling, and resting, they interact with each other and with their environment. These connections between living things have shaped the natural world. Sadly, we are making survival increasingly difficult for wildlife. As people clear the land for their own uses, they force animals out of places where they once lived, and some species are being wiped out by hunters and trappers. Many wild animals are becoming scarcer year by year, and thousands are in danger of extinction.

Since the beginning of time, different animal species have come and gone naturally, like the dinosaurs did. But in the coming years, extinction rates may be 10,000 times above normal.

"Twenty-five percent of all species could vanish within 20 years."

THOMAS LOVEJOY, CHIEF BIODIVERSITY ADVISER FOR THE WORLD BANK, 2000

Saving animals is not always easy, but the good news is that there are lots of people and organizations working to find solutions. We can all take steps to learn about animals' needs and help with wildlife conservation, but we still have a long way to go. On some of the main issues, such as rain forest protection and safari hunting, experts do not always agree on the problems or what should be done. This book explains both sides of the arguments, giving us a clear picture of what is at stake.

Because so many animals are at risk, it is easy to feel there is little we can do. But individuals can make a difference. In this book, there are suggestions for ways you can play an active role, and experiments to provide firsthand experience of some of the scientific issues. Day in the Life journals describe the work of experts in the field, while letters from young people around the world reveal their concerns for the environment. If we act now, we can help to safeguard the future of the world's wildlife.

HABITATS
AT RISK

AN ANIMAL'S HABITAT IS THE PLACE THAT PROVIDES IT WITH FOOD, WATER, AND SHELTER. BUT HUMAN ACTIVITY IS AFFECTING HABITATS AROUND the world, altering the landscape, poisoning the air and water, and disturbing the balance of living things. As environments are changed, animal populations are suffering. By protecting habitats we can protect the animals that live there.

Animals are adapted to live in a particular environment. All sorts of animals, including elephants and impalas (main picture), thrive on African grasslands. If habitats change, animals may not be able to survive in the new conditions. When natural fires sweep across the South American home of the giant anteater (right), the vegetation slowly grows back. But when people light fires to clear the land for farming, the anteater loses its home for good.

"...habitat loss has reduced many populations to such low levels that they are unlikely to survive beyond another few generations."

GLOBAL ENVIRONMENT FACILITY, 1998

Birds may fly accidentally into overhead wires or windowpanes, often with tragic results.

> **"...one-quarter of the world's mammal species are now at risk of extinction."**
>
> KLAUS TÖPFER, UNITED NATIONS ENVIRONMENT PROGRAM, 1999

NOWHERE
to live

New hazards
Some creatures have adapted well to life in built-up areas. The British barn owl has found that roadsides make good hunting sites, but 3,000 of them are killed on roads every year. The modern world is full of unnatural hazards for animals, such as fast-moving vehicles and farm machinery.

American black bears have resorted to raiding the garbage dumps on the edges of their woodland homes.

For wildlife across the world, finding somewhere to feed, rest, and breed can be a struggle. All through history, people have altered the environments in which they live, clearing trees and riverbanks, erecting buildings, planting crops, and digging up minerals. Today, the scale and pace of change is alarming. More and more land is being converted into towns, farms, roads, and factories. As their habitats shrink, animal populations decrease and some species face extinction. However, special areas are now being set aside for the protection of habitats, and there is much we can do to help animals survive alongside us.

Shrinking wilderness
American black bears have learned to look in unusual places for food as their natural supplies run out. As human settlements expand, they take up spaces where wild animals once roamed free. Some animals can adapt to slight changes in their habitat, but few can survive when roads and houses start to take over the landscape.

By **learning** more about how we **affect** the environment we can **learn** how best to **safeguard** it for the **future**

Big meat-eaters at the top of the food chain need large habitats in which to find enough prey.

The **protection** of **endangered** animal **species** almost always involves the **protection** of their **habitats** too

ACTION!
HELP ANIMALS

Fit a nest box to a tree or wall in your garden to give birds a secure place to rear their young.

Never pick flowers or take anything away with you when visiting the countryside. It could be part of an animal's home.

Predators need prey

Farms and ranches are intruding on the hunting territories of African wild dogs – and their natural prey is diminishing. When wild animals cannot find enough of their natural prey, they may attack domestic cattle or sheep instead, bringing them into conflict with people. Many are then shot by farmers.

Squeezed out

The Australian broad-headed snake is one of many species at risk of dying out because of severe damage to its habitats. This snake's last remaining refuges are being ruined because people are taking the rocks under which it shelters to decorate their gardens.

Wild waterside plants offer food and shelter.

The broad-headed snake lives in just one small area in Southeast Australia.

Making space

Even within built-up areas, it is possible to help wild animals to survive. Digging a backyard pond, for example, creates a haven for freshwater creatures including frogs, newts, diving beetles, and dragonflies. The animals will have a place to breed, and frogs will return year after year to mate and lay their eggs.

Helping hand

Ospreys nest on the tops of old bare trees near water. Where such trees have been cut down, tall poles topped with platforms can provide artificial nest sites. People can take steps like this to help animals survive in disrupted habitats. Providing alternative sources of food can also be helpful when natural supplies are low.

70 percent of the Earth's surface

TROUBLED

Dam landscape

The Balbina Dam in Brazil is one of many dam projects around the world that has flooded huge areas of land upstream. Built to generate electric power, Balbina submerged a vast area of Amazon rain forest.

Scarlet macaw
A new dam project could flood some of the last remaining breeding sites of the scarlet macaw in Belize.

Animal rescue
Efforts to rescue trapped animals, such as this sloth in Brazil, only save a fraction of the flood victims.

Wetlands and rivers are among the most vulnerable of all wildlife habitats. They are places where the needs of people and the needs of wild animals often clash. Unfortunately for wildlife, valleys, coasts, and low-lying plains are just where people like to live. As they interfere with rivers to provide power, control flooding, and allow boats to pass through, people make life hard for animals. By draining marshes, swamps, and mudflats to make space for farms and coastal developments, people destroy the precious refuges of the creatures whose lives depend on these wetlands.

February 2nd is World Wetlands Day, when money is raised to protect the world's rivers and lakes

Flood victims

As the waters rise behind a dam, they break the banks of the old river and spill out across the valley floor to form a reservoir. An entire landscape becomes permanently flooded, and all the animals that belonged there lose their homes. Many drown before they can escape.

is covered with water
WATERS

River disruption

The common sturgeon is in trouble because dams in many of its European rivers prevent it from moving upstream to breed. Dams also disrupt habitats downstream. They alter water levels and water quality in the river, making it less suitable for many aquatic animals.

Swamp life

Tropical mangrove swamps are havens for creatures like this mudskipper – a fish that can breathe out of water. They also provide safe habitats for young fish and nest sites for seabirds. Many swamps are being destroyed to make space for shrimp farms.

This butterfly was once extinct in Britain, but has now been reintroduced to some areas of the country.

Drained out

Marshland animals like the European large copper butterfly are suffering the world over because many countries have lost most of their freshwater marshes. People dig ditches to drain the low-lying wetlands and create flat land for farming and building.

ACTION!
FIND OUT

Join a local group that campaigns to protect rivers and wetlands in the area where you live.

Try to arrange a visit with friends, family, or school to see the wildlife on a protected area of wetland near your home.

Waterdock, the food plant of the large copper's caterpillars, thrives in marshland.

Fish ladder

Dam builders sometimes add "fish ladders" to their designs, as shown here at the Bonneville Dam on the Columbia River in the Pacific Northwest. Fish such as salmon can leap up the steps, down which water cascades. This allows them to migrate past the dam to their spawning grounds and continue breeding.

More than half the world's freshwater vertebrates are in decline

WETLANDS MANAGER
MICHAEL MITCHELL

MICHAEL MITCHELL'S JOB AS A WETLANDS MANAGER FOR THE UNITED STATES FISH AND WILDLIFE SERVICE HELPS HIM TO MAKE HIS DREAM OF SAVING HABITATS FOR ANIMALS come true. Each day he must decide what is best for the wildlife in the Eastern Shore of Virginia National Wildlife Refuge – an area of marshy grassland on the Atlantic coast of Virginia.

A day in the life of a
WETLANDS MANAGER

Michael protects wild animals in their natural environment – the information he gathers will help conservationists all over the world.

Today, Michael will meet a variety of animals on the wetland refuge he runs. He cares for the whole habitat, and all the animals that live there or pass through.

Angry falcon
Peregrine falcons tend to bite, but Michael does not wear gloves to avoid causing injury to the bird.

8:00am It is November – the time of year when hawks and falcons are migrating south. Our task this morning is to tag them so that we can monitor their migration routes. First we position nets around a pigeon to attract passing hawks and falcons, who will think that it is an easy meal. Just as a peregrine falcon hits the net, I run to place a numbered band on his leg before releasing him to continue on his way. If the bird is caught again at another banding station, or if the band is found under other circumstances, the information will help our understanding of migration.

9:00am Another of my jobs is to help woodcocks to survive the cold winter by creating grassy areas where they can find earthworms. Using a big mower called a "bush-hog," I cut strips through the bush to give the birds better access to the ground. Woodcocks are odd-looking animals, with round

Powerful flashlight allows Michael to work at night.

Net is used to catch birds without causing injury.

All-terrain
Michael's truck is adapted to carry him and his equipment about the refuge.

bodies, skinny legs, and long, thin beaks. They have a funny habit of rocking back and forth – possibly using their sensitive feet to detect earthworms moving under the ground. Tonight, when the birds are feeding at the prepared site, with the help of the spotlights on the all-terrain vehicle, we will use nets to catch the birds. We will then weigh, measure,

and band them for study – observing and monitoring the animals on the wetland refuge is an important part of my job.

11:00am White-tailed deer are beautiful animals, and one of the least pleasant parts of my job is to manage a hunt that reduces the number of deer on the refuge.

Important wetlands
The wetlands that Michael and his team care for support a wide range of animals. Wetlands also filter pollution from the rivers that flow through them.

Creatures from the sea
It is part of Michael's job to care for, and protect, the animals that live off the coast of the refuge.

This job is necessary because deer can quickly breed and multiply to numbers that cause overcrowding. This results in disease and starvation. A hunter brings in two males, or bucks. I weigh them and work out their age from the number and condition of their teeth. I also check for signs of disease. In this way, the hunting helps us in our management. It allows close-up inspections that can turn up problems in the herd that might otherwise go unseen. I issue the hunters with a certificate to say that the deer were legally taken.

2:00pm A distress call from a boater reports a loggerhead sea turtle having trouble swimming. Quickly, I

throw a net and a blanket into my truck and call the Virginia Institute of Marine Science (VIMS) to ask for their help. I find the disabled turtle and, with the help of the boaters, we net her and gently move her to shore. I suspect she is suffering from cold-shock, a common problem at this time of year. We wrap the turtle in the blanket and move her to the warm truck. When the VIMS volunteers arrive, they take the animal to their indoor tanks to feed, treat, and nurture her back to health. Within a few weeks, the turtle should have recovered and will be released in the warmer waters of South Carolina. All the turtle needs is some warmth and care to help her to recover from the cold-shock that paralyzed her.

4:00pm Butterfly researcher Mark Garland and I set off to Fisherman Island, a 2,000-acre (800-hectare) reserve, to see if any monarch

" In the fall, the sky above the refuge is filled with thousands and thousands of migrating birds. **"**

butterflies are resting there on their migration south. We search the island and find no butterflies. But, as we are about to leave, we spot a strange-looking, orange-colored tree. It is covered by thousands of butterflies. All of the butterflies on the island are in one clump, hanging from one tree, maybe because it is in a particularly sheltered spot. We place a small numbered paper tag on one wing of 20 butterflies, then leave them to rest for the night. The monarchs will fly on to central Mexico. If researchers there find our tags, they will learn that the butterflies spent a night enjoying

Mass of monarchs
Migrating monarch butterflies cluster together to keep warm as they rest.

the hospitality of our tree. Details like this add to our knowledge of butterfly migration. All I have to do now is to record the details of my day, so that the information can be used in the future.

Save the turtle
Loggerhead sea turtles are endangered. People from all over the world are combining efforts to save this and other species of sea turtle.

"There are fewer insects now than at any time since mankind has been on this planet."

GORDON RAMEL
ENTOMOLOGIST, 1998

Micro-life

Life on land is dominated by small creatures. Animals such as insects, spiders, and worms – as well as some too small to see – are all around us. Insects alone make up about 65 percent of all the animal species so far identified. And, like all living things, they need safe, suitable habitats for survival. As humans disrupt habitats across the globe, some micro-life is threatened just as many larger animals are. Small creatures sustain life on this planet by pollinating plants, decomposing waste, and providing food for larger animals. Their survival is vital to the well-being of all other life.

Important partners

The yucca plant cannot survive without the yucca moth. It relies on the moth to carry its pollen from flower to flower. Pollination is vital because this is what makes plants able to produce seed. Many small animals help plants to survive. For example, bees also spread pollen, and earthworms make the soil looser and better for plant growth.

ACTION!
HELP INSECTS

Find out which plants are food for caterpillars and grow them in your yard to attract butterflies.

Make a compost heap in your yard with organic waste. It will become home to many creatures.

Many of the **plants** that provide us with **food** and materials rely on **insects** to **pollinate** them

Newly cut sweet chestnut coppice.

Threatened species

The great raft spider and the giant dung beetle are two known micro-life victims of habitat loss. Other small creatures that are threatened include species of ants and earthworms. Scientists think some micro-life becomes extinct before it is even discovered.

Great raft spider
Drainage and disruption of fens and marshes are a threat to this large species of northern European water-loving spider.

Dung beetle
As the wild buffalo of southern Africa has become more rare, so has the dung beetle that lays eggs in its dung.

Ninety percent of all **plant** material is **broken down** and **recycled** by **earthworms** and other **decomposers**

Emperor dragonfly
This dragonfly's waterside breeding grounds are not as widespread as they once were.

Sensitive to change

Coppicing is when woodland trees are regularly cut so that lots of thin shoots grow from the tree stumps. These shoots make good fence poles and also create ideal conditions for some small animals. Coppices are not as common as they once were, and species such as fritillary butterflies have declined as a result.

Conservation target

Micro-life is not often the target of conservation projects. In southwest England, however, the Royal Society for the Protection of Birds (RSPB) is working to protect the waterside habitats of the emperor dragonfly. The RSPB has created artificial wetlands to provide places for the dragonflies and other small animals to breed and feed.

MAKE A WORMERY
EXPERIMENT

You will need: a glass bowl, protective gloves, some dark soil and silver sand, leaves, water, earthworms, paper, adhesive tape.

1 **SPRINKLE LAYERS OF DARK SOIL** and silver sand into the bowl until it is almost full. Place small pieces of leaves on top and moisten the soil with water.

2 **DIG UP SOME EARTHWORMS FROM** the yard and put them on the soil. Place paper with holes over the container and secure it with adhesive tape. Place somewhere cool and dark.

The tunnels made by the worms are visible through the glass.

3 **CHECK THE WORMERY** every day and keep it damp. After a few days you will see that the layers are mixing up and the leaves have been pulled into the soil.

This shows that: as worms tunnel, they circulate air and materials through the soil. This is vital for making soil more fertile for plants. Remember to put the worms back in the yard when the experiment is over.

Forty percent of the world's species of plants and animals live in **rain forests**

FOREST HOMES

From the top of the trees to the leaf-strewn floor, forests provide homes for an amazing variety of wildlife. The existence of the trees is vital to the survival of countless species that rely on them for food and shelter. Yet forests across the world have been steadily shrinking in size. People chop down trees for firewood and light fires to make way for other uses of the land. Trees are also cut down for timber, which is exported all over the world. Logging for timber does not have to be destructive. Some forests are managed in a sustainable way that reduces damage and allows trees to regrow.

Rain forest loss

Every year, farmers set fire to huge areas of tropical rain forest to clear the land for crops, as here in South America. Many of the farmers are poor and in desperate need of new land. But the gradual destruction of rain forests is worrying because many of the animals that live there cannot survive outside the forest environment.

High-rise habitat

Just as people live in buildings, woodland animals, like the red squirrel, make their homes in trees. A tree is rather like an apartment block, with different animals living on different floors. The squirrel spends most of its time high in the treetops. Other animals prefer the shady lower branches, and some set up home in the soil beneath.

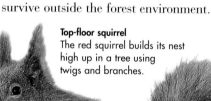

Top-floor squirrel
The red squirrel builds its nest high up in a tree using twigs and branches.

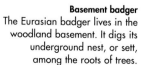

Basement badger
The Eurasian badger lives in the woodland basement. It digs its underground nest, or sett, among the roots of trees.

"I live in St. Asaph near Clocaenog Forest in Wales. The forest attracts many visitors — and not just people! During a school visit we found that there are lots of animals living deep within the sanctuary of the forest, including red squirrels and black grouse, which are now rare in Britain. Special rangers look after the forest and the animals. They plant new trees to replace ones that have been cut down for wood, and put up boxes for bats to nest in. I think it is fantastic that animals can live in the forest in peace."

K. A. Daly

Forest dependents

Logging is destroying the forest homes of the orangutan and has driven the Leadbeater's opossum and many other animals close to extinction. Creatures like these are dependent on trees – they provide their nesting and resting places. Trees also absorb nutrients from the forest floor and turn them into plentiful food supplies, such as leaves, nuts, and fruit. Trees are the life supports of the forest, and forest animals have evolved to live among them.

Leadbeater's opossum
This little Australian mammal nests in tall, aging trees and has only fragments of suitable habitat remaining.

Conserving trees

This man is placing a cup on a rubber tree to collect the sap, called latex, that is dripping from a score he made in the bark. In forests like this one in Brazil, where the trees are left standing, local people harvest products such as rubber, nuts, and honey. This means the forests are protected, and the people can still make a living from them.

Long, strong fingers are specially adapted for life in the trees.

Fewer than 30,000 **orangutans** remain **in the wild** in the **forests** of Borneo and **Sumatra**

Orangutan
These apes move clumsily on the ground. They are the only great apes that spend most of their time in the trees.

ACTION!
SAVE TREES

Find out if you can join in with any clean-up projects that are going on in a wooded area or forest near you.

Don't waste paper – write or draw on both sides.

Take your wastepaper and cardboard to a local recycling center.

Perils of POLLUTION

Day after day, chemicals flush into rivers, gases seep into the air, and waste is strewn on the land. The planet is being contaminated for all living things. Pollution is often invisible, but it can do as much damage to habitats as flames and bulldozers. Pollution weakens animals by poisoning their food supplies. Poisons, or toxins, build up in an animal's body until they reach dangerous levels.

For species already suffering from habitat disruption, pollution of their remaining home can be devastating. Some people are now finding alternatives to chemical pesticides, and using energy from sources which do not produce harmful waste, such as solar and wind power.

Deadly damage

After an oil spill at sea, oil washes up onto beaches, as here in Texas. Oil can cause problems for wildlife before it is cleared up, killing many seabirds and sand-dwelling creatures. The oil clogs up feathers and fur, and poisons animals if it enters their bodies.

Chemical contamination

Top predators, such as bald eagles, suffer when their prey is contaminated with toxins. Pollution is not always an accident. Some factories release chemicals into the air and rivers, and farmers' pesticides poison wildlife on land and in the water. Since the pesticide DDT was banned, bald eagle populations are recovering.

Failed eggs

These sparrowhawk eggs were too fragile to develop because of harmful pesticides consumed by the parent birds. Today, pesticides are often made from plant extracts, and are kinder to the environment than those based on artificial chemicals.

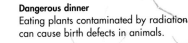
Dangerous dinner
Eating plants contaminated by radiation can cause birth defects in animals.

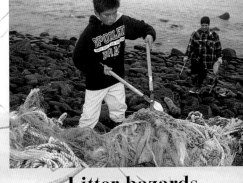

Radiation
The pastures of wild reindeer and farm animals were contaminated after a nuclear accident at the Chernobyl power station in the Ukraine, in 1986. Reindeer in Lapland ate contaminated moss, and many had to be slaughtered. Severe radioactive pollution is rare, but its effects on animals can be disastrous.

Litter hazards
Organized clean-up projects make places like this beach in Alaska look better and also remove hazards for wildlife. Litter, such as discarded fishing nets, lead weights, and plastic yokes that hold soda cans, can entangle, poison, and strangle wild animals.

Fighting pollution
Environmental groups, such as Greenpeace, campaign to stop people from polluting the environment. In 1996, members of Greenpeace protested about the Brent Spar oil platform which was going to be dumped on the ocean bed. They claimed that the structure was full of toxic materials. The protest helped to change disposal plans for all oil and gas rigs in the area.

LONG-TERM LITTER
EXPERIMENT

You will need: two empty jelly jars, protective gloves, damp soil collected from outside, a thin slice of apple, a square of aluminum foil, a small piece from a plastic bag, a large sheet of paper.

1 FILL THE JELLY JARS HALF FULL with soil. Put the slice of apple in one, and the square of foil and piece of plastic in the other. Cover them with soil and leave the jars in a warm place.

Substances like foil and plastic may take hundreds of years to decompose.

2 AFTER A WEEK, EMPTY the contents of both jars onto the paper. You will see that the apple has begun to shrivel up and decay, but the foil and the plastic look like new.

This shows that: tiny organisms in soil break down natural waste, but litter made from metal and plastic does not decompose easily. It can stay in the environment for a long time, harming generations of wildlife.

WILDLIFE VET
ANDREW ROUTH

ANDREW ROUTH HAS BEEN A VETERINARY SURGEON FOR ALMOST 20 YEARS. HE BECAME A VET BECAUSE OF HIS INTEREST IN WILDLIFE, AND NOW treats injured and abandoned animals, and returns them to their natural homes. Unlike pets, wild animals are not used to being handled and can be difficult to care for.

A day in the life of a
WILDLIFE VET

Many of the sick and injured animals that Andrew treats are suffering as a result of human carelessness.

Fox cub on a dripfeed
Wild animals often reach the hospital in a state of shock. Putting them on a drip feed helps them to recover by replacing lost fluids.

Today, Andrew is working for the Royal Society for the Prevention of Cruelty to Animals (RSPCA) in its Wildlife Hospital in King's Lynn, UK. He works all over the world, and no two days are the same.

8:30am I arrive at the hospital. The staff on the morning shift report that there were no problems overnight, despite the fact that there are more than 250 animals in the hospital. I check on the patients in the isolation wing. There is a fox cub on a dripfeed, a young swan that crash-landed on a road, and more than 12 seal pups. Many of the seal pups were washed up on the beach and must be handreared.

9:15am My first job is to check some droppings from a young otter in our care. He was caught helping himself to some expensive fish in

Microscope

Spraint (otter dropping)

Young otter
Hunting and habitat loss put UK otter populations in danger, but otters are now protected and starting to recover.

a garden pond. This was not normal otter behavior, and blood tests showed that he was ill. I use a microscope to look for parasite eggs in his droppings. Fortunately, there are none, so we can let him join the other

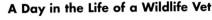

Hands on
By carefully feeling the swan all over, Andrew can tell whether she has any injuries, or if she is underweight.

NORTH SEA

UNITED KINGDOM

IRELAND

King's Lynn
NORFOLK
Cambridge
London

ENGLISH CHANNEL

Tawny owl
Handling wild birds distresses them, so it is common to make them go to sleep, or anaesthetize them, before they are examined. The bird breathes the anaesthetic through a special mask.

young otters before he is returned to the wild. He has finished his antibiotics, and his second blood test is clear. Checking droppings may not sound exciting, but otters are still quite rare in the UK, and I get an extra thrill at being able to contribute to their conservation.

10:30am An RSPCA inspector brings in a swan that was found on the bank of a river. Like many swans, she may have swallowed a lead weight left by an angler. I take an X-ray, and my suspicions are confirmed. A veterinary nurse helps me take a blood sample, then I inject the swan with a drug that will help it to get rid of the lead from its body. Swans with lead poisoning often have to spend several weeks in the hospital.

12:15pm A member of the public turns up with a tawny owl found by a road. His left wing is drooping. Like so many of our patients he has been hit by a car. With a veterinary nurse assisting, I give a general anesthetic to the owl. We find that a bone in his wing is broken. All being well, the bandage I apply will give the bone a chance to heal.

> 66 Seeing the animals I have treated back in the wild is the best reward I could have for my work. 99

2:00pm A number of birds in the aviaries need a health check before they are released. These are birds that arrived, like the tawny owl, with injuries. But they are now well on the road to recovery. Putting them in the aviaries gives them room to fly and get fit for survival back in the wild. The largest bird is a buzzard, which is now strong enough to injure me when I catch him. I am particularly interested in one kestrel. This bird of prey hunts by sight for small rodents, and it is vital that I examine his eyes. He gets the all clear and, as this

bird was found locally, we can take him to the release site. He leaves my hands like a bullet, and we then see him hovering over some rough grassland.

5:00pm A hedgehog is brought in. She was found during the day – something we do not expect from a nocturnal animal. When she breathes I can hear a rattling noise from her chest. This suggests that she has pneumonia caused by lungworm. She will need to double her weight before she can hibernate through the approaching UK winter. That should be it for the day, but the hospital never closes, and tonight I am the vet on call.

Close inspection
Andrew wears gloves when handling hedgehogs, because they often carry fleas and ringworm.

Variety of life
With the North Sea close at hand, and large areas of open countryside, Norfolk is home to a wide variety of animals.

11:30pm The local badger group telephones the hospital to say they have an injured badger. They are bringing him to the hospital, and I go to meet them. The badger has been injured by a car while crossing the road. He is badly stunned and has a head wound, but no other injuries. He responds well to a drip. I give him painkilling drugs and sedatives to relax him, and he is hospitalized so that the night-shift can keep an eye on him for me. Now I know who my first patient will be in the morning.

The badger is made warm and comfortable and left to recover.

Badger accident
For nocturnal animals like badgers, roads can be dangerous.

"If enough Arctic ice is lost, polar bears will become extinct."

WWF GLOBAL NETWORK, 1999

At the limits

The cool mountaintops in the Cape region of South Africa are home to rare stag beetles. If global warming continues, mountain animals may have to move higher to find the right conditions. But these beetles already live on the summit – they have nowhere to go.

Climate

change

Emperor geese nest on the Yukon Delta in Alaska, one of many wildlife refuges at risk from a rise in sea levels.

ACTION!
SAVE ENERGY

Switch off lights when you leave a room.

Reuse plastic carrier bags – making plastic uses a lot of energy.

Ask if low-energy lightbulbs can be used at home and at school.

The buildup of polluting gases in the atmosphere is slowly changing the weather patterns on Earth. For example, we are producing too much carbon dioxide when we burn fuel like wood, coal, and oil. This is collecting with other gases to form a "blanket" around the Earth. The blanket is stopping heat from escaping into space, and the temperature on Earth is rising. Many wild animals are already feeling the effect of this global warming. Some countries are trying to make people use less energy so that less fuel is burned.

Threatened refuges

If global warming continues, areas set aside for the protection of wetland birds, such as the emperor goose, may be ruined. Higher temperatures make water expand and melt polar ice, so sea levels rise. Coastal nesting sites of millions of birds may soon be flooded.

Polar bears hunt on ice in the winter and eat little for the rest of the year. Now that the ice is melting earlier, the bears are starting the summer without enough fat stored to keep them healthy.

Moving mosquito
Mosquitos can spread diseases like malaria when they bite. Cases of malaria in new places suggest that the *Anopheles* mosquito is starting to spread beyond its normal range because of climate change.

Shifting range

As land and sea temperatures rise, many wildlife species will be on the move. Tropical animals may advance into areas that were once too chilly for them. Cold-loving animals will have to move nearer the poles to find cooler habitats. Some creatures, such as the mosquito, are already extending their habitats to include the new, warm areas.

Lemon sole
Ocean warming may force this fish to start moving to cooler waters. Changes like this could disrupt food chains, causing some species to decline.

The way in which certain **gases** in the atmosphere **trap heat** is known as the greenhouse effect

ANIMAL INSULATION

EXPERIMENT

You will need: 2 identical jelly jars with lids, rolled cotton, adhesive tape, warm tap water.

1 FILL ONE OF THE JELLY JARS WITH WARM tap water. Put the lid on, and cover it all over with a thick layer of rolled cotton, held in place with adhesive tape. (The cotton is a substitute for fur.) Fill the other jar with warm tap water. Put the lid on, but leave it uncovered.

You can add food dye to the water to make the experiment more colorful.

2 LEAVE THE JARS for about half an hour, and then dip your finger in both to test the warmth of the water. The water in the covered jar has stayed warm, but the water in the other jar has cooled down.

Heat escapes easily through the uninsulated glass.

This shows that: dense fur keeps warmth in. This is important in a very cold climate but, if the weather warms up, it could make an Arctic animal overheat dangerously.

Warming effects

Polar bears are adapted to cold, Arctic conditions and cannot survive well in warm environments. They already seem to be suffering from climate change, partly because the seals on which they prey have been affected. Ringed seals are having trouble breeding because the snow caves where they rear their pups are melting and collapsing too early in the year.

Giant African land snail
This huge snail, reared on Pacific islands as a source of food, escaped into the wild and soon became a serious crop pest.

Alien arrival
The giant African land snail and the *Euglandina* snail were introduced to the Pacific islands of Tahiti and Moorea, in both cases with disastrous results. Alien animals can be introduced in different ways. *Euglandina* was released on purpose. But some animals, like the land snail, escape from captivity, and others arrive by accident, often hidden in ships' cargo.

Snail-eating snail
To reduce the number of giant African land snails, the *Euglandina rosea* was released on the Pacific islands.

Native snail
Sadly, several species of Pacific *Partula* snails were driven to extinction by the newcomer, *Euglandina rosea*.

Even introduced pets, like cats and dogs, can put native wildlife at risk

New species, NEW THREATS

The release of an animal into a habitat where it does not belong can be destructive for the creatures that already live there. Although wild animals are able to share their home with certain other animals, the introduction of a newcomer, or "alien" species, can upset nature's balance. An invader is often too powerful a predator or too greedy a consumer of vegetation. The threat from introduced animals is especially serious on islands where wildlife has evolved in isolation. Many of these vulnerable island species are now carefully protected.

Fearsome foxes
In Australia, introduced foxes prey on rare mammals such as the numbat, the bilby, and the stick-nest rat.

No escape
Predatory mammals such as foxes, stoats, rats, and domestic cats are some of the most destructive animals that have been introduced into new habitats. Island creatures often evolve with few natural predators and are not able to hide, run, or fly away.

Hungry stoats
The arrival of stoats in New Zealand almost spelled doom for the takahe, a large but flightless native bird.

Stowaway rats
Black rats have spread around the world by climbing ships' moorings and hiding on board.

Shelter is becoming hard to find for the rhinoceros iguana.

Nowhere to hide

Native species, such as the rhinoceros iguana of Hispaniola, can be affected when large farm animals are allowed to roam free. In many areas on the island, the scrubby thickets where the iguana likes to hide, are now eaten and trampled by introduced donkeys and goats.

New competitors

The greater bilby has been driven from parts of Australia by the spread of introduced rabbits, which take over its burrows. Like rabbits, some alien animals harm native wildlife, not by preying on them, but by competing with them for food and shelter.

Alien animals often feed on the eggs and young of native species

The kakapo feeds at night, when predators are less likely to spot it.

66 I live on Maud Island, a refuge for kakapo in New Zealand. There are 18 kakapo on the island, which is free of predators such as cats, stoats, and dogs. When I first met Hoki, the hand-reared kakapo, I sat down quietly and she nibbled on my fingers and chucked sticks at me. At night she would climb onto our roof and it sounded like she was jumping up and down. Hoki was moved to Codfish Island to live in the wild. I haven't seen her since. She has not laid her first eggs yet, but I hope she will have some chicks of her own. 99 *Samantha Paton*

Genetic mixing

A different sort of threat faces the rare Simien wolf of Ethiopia. Domestic dogs that have become wild have entered some of the wolf's last remaining refuges, and the two closely related animals have started to breed with each other. Over time, this mixing of genes could mean that the true Simien wolf disappears.

Intensive rescue

New Zealand's large, flightless parrot, the kakapo, has been rescued from the brink of extinction. The few remaining birds have been moved from the mainland to nearby islands, where they are safer from predators and can be monitored by conservationists. Measures like this have saved a number of island species from extinction.

HUNTING
AND TRADE

MANY WILD ANIMALS FACE A DOUBLE THREAT. NOT ONLY ARE THEY LOSING THEIR HABITATS, BUT THEY ARE ALSO TARGETS for exploitation. Across the world, people hunt and capture wildlife, sometimes to feed and clothe their families. More often it is to sell the meat and other products, or to trade the live animals for money.

" Many of the world's most precious and best-loved species are being traded into oblivion. **"**

ALAN THORNTON
CHAIRMAN OF ENVIRONMENTAL
INVESTIGATION AGENCY, 1994

Hunting can take a terrible toll on wildlife species such as the tiger (main picture). Much of the trade in furs (inset) and body parts of endangered animals is now against the law. Plenty of people are still prepared to poach, smuggle, and buy these illegal goods.

Overhunted animal populations can usually **recover** if their natural **habitats** are not **damaged**

Animal HARVEST

ACTION!
SAVE WILDLIFE

Support organizations that work to reduce the impact of unmanaged hunting.

Adopt an animal that has been orphaned, through a wildlife group such as the Worldwide Fund for Nature.

Throughout history, people have hunted animals for food. At first, the harvest of wildlife had little effect on animal populations because, like other predators, humans were few in number. But as towns and cities expanded and commercial hunting became common, the pressure on wild animals increased. Most meat today comes from domesticated, farmed animals, but hunting for food is still important for people in some countries. Where species are threatened, conservationists are trying to persuade people to change their sources of food and to limit hunting so that animals are not killed faster than they breed.

Feeding families
Wild antelopes called duikers are a common source of meat for people in Central Africa. Hunting for "bushmeat" like this poses a threat to wildlife, from crocodiles to chimpanzees. Hunters take wild animals to feed their families or to sell. In places, areas of forest have been picked clean of edible creatures.

Easy target
The Victoria crowned pigeon of New Guinea is under threat because it is hunted for its flesh. At up to 31.5 in (80 cm) long, this plump bird is the world's largest pigeon. Because it spends most of its time foraging on the forest floor, it is an easy target for hunters.

The sea turns red after a roundup of pilot whales.

Ritual slaughter

Every year, people drive schools of pilot whales into shallow bays around the Faroe Islands, north of Scotland, for mass slaughter. In the past, these annual events provided a much-needed food source for the islanders. Today there are plenty of alternatives, but many islanders are eager to continue the traditional hunt.

Wildlife farming

Ostriches are commonly bred for their meat in southern Africa, and ostrich farms are now springing up in other parts of the world. This type of animal harvest does not harm wild populations and is better than taking animals from their natural habitats.

Poached eggs

In Southeast Asia, river turtles called batagurs are caught for their flesh when they come out of the water to lay their eggs. Hunters also dig up the eggs to eat, destroying a whole new generation of these endangered reptiles. Many beaches and riverbanks are now protected during the breeding season.

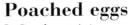
Chicks must be fed a balanced diet to ensure that they grow properly.

Iguanas, hunted for food in Central America, are now bred in captivity to sustain wild populations

Saved in time

Native Americans hunted bison in North America for thousands of years. Then, in the 19th century, European settlers almost wiped out the animal – a population of 60 million was reduced to 1,000. A few herds were saved, and numbers steadily increased. Today, there are more than 20,000.

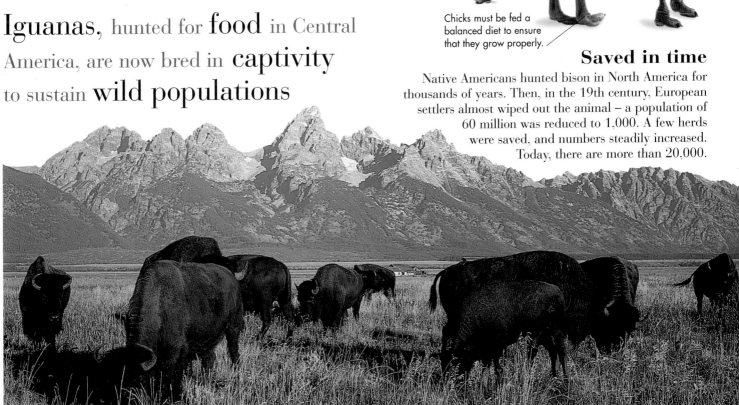

Sustainable fishing could provide a constantly renewable source of food

Too Few Fish

The seas and freshwater habitats of the world yield millions of tons of fish and shellfish. Fish are our most important harvest from the wild. But no matter how huge the expanses of water may seem, fish stocks are not inexhaustible. If we take too much from the seas and rivers, fish populations can collapse. This not only threatens fish and shellfish species, but also affects other animals that depend on them for food. Controls on fishing have been introduced to try to make the industry more sustainable and protect aquatic wildlife.

Mackerel
This fish is an easy catch, because it feeds at the water's surface.

Collapse of a fishery
Overfishing of species such as mackerel can make stocks so scarce that fishing boats can no longer find enough fish to fill their nets. As fishing technology has advanced, fish populations have been exploited on an enormous scale around the world. International agreements on catch sizes are becoming ever more necessary.

Mekong catfish rarely reach their **full size** of 6.5 ft (2 m) because so **many** are caught when they are **young**

Freshwater victims
The pirarucu is a prized food fish along the Amazon River, but it is now rare in many areas. Part of the reason for this rapid decline is that hunters do not always fish with nets or lines. They sometimes resort to blasting the pirarucus out of the water with dynamite, or shooting them with rifles.

Threatened shellfish
Some shellfish are affected by overfishing. The giant clam has been plundered close to extinction along many island coasts in the western Pacific Ocean. Other prized mollusks, such as conch, are also intensively fished for their flesh. Even common crustaceans like crabs and lobsters will suffer if people continue to raid the seas.

Sardines, haddock, herrings, and anchovies have all been victims of **overfishing**

> # "Scientists are breeding corals to be transplanted to damaged reefs."
>
> KEITH HAMMOND, AQUACULTURIST

Destructive methods

Dynamite blasting along coral reefs, like these in the Philippines, destroys sections of the reef and kills many species of fish. The dead fish can then be gathered from the water. The use of long drift nets is another fishing method that kills non-target species, such as sea turtles and dolphins.

Ecological impacts

Overfishing can seriously affect other animals. Heavy fishing of sand eels around the Shetland Islands off Scotland is thought to have caused problems at the islands' puffin colonies. Chicks appear to have starved to death due to a shortage of sand eels.

ACTION!
PROTECT FISH

Follow local rules if you go fishing, and look after your catch until you let it go.

Try to buy "dolphin friendly" canned fish.

Buy fresh fish, such as trout, that comes from farms rather than from rivers or the sea.

Fishing patrols

Official fishing patrols, such as this one along a coral reef in the Philippines, are a useful weapon in the fight against illegal fishing. The patrols try to stop people from using dynamite-blast fishing, and check catches to make sure that rules on species and catch sizes are not broken. In some places, the fishing communities themselves organize patrols.

"Trade in tiger bone threatens to drive this animal to extinction."

KRISTIN NOWELL, TRAFFIC, 1999

Parts for SALE

ACTION!
SHOP WISELY

Avoid buying shells or other animal products as vacation souvenirs.

Contact an organization that works to prevent trade in rare animal parts, and see if you can do something to help.

Look out for soaps and shampoos that do not contain rare animal products.

Many animals are not hunted for food, but for their skin, fur, horns, shells, or other body parts. These animal parts are traded far and wide as decorative objects, ingredients for traditional medicines, or materials for the fashion industry. The wild victims of such trade include many highly endangered species such as big cats, rhinoceroses, gorillas, crocodiles, and sea turtles. Some governments around the world have now made laws to try to control the trade in animal products, but these laws are not easy to enforce.

The cost of fashion

Until recently, rare chinchillas from the mountains of South America were trapped for their soft fur, which was used to decorate clothes. The demand for fur still has a terrible effect on many scarce wild mammals. Some animals are raised in captivity for their fur, but anti-fur campaigners argue that these animals still suffer cruel treatment.

Traditional medicine

Animals including Asiatic black bears and tigers are in danger, due to the demands of traditional medicines. Hunters kill bears to collect their gall bladders and other body parts, for use in traditional potions. People are now more aware of the illegal trade in animal parts, thanks to the work of organizations such as TRAFFIC. This group aims to ensure that wildlife species are not traded to extinction.

Red fox
With its leg held in a trap, this fox could suffer hours of pain, thirst, hunger, and exposure.

Golden eagle
Rare birds of prey, such as golden eagles, are often caught in traps by mistake.

" I live in Chicago, where I am proud to be a young member of PETA (People for the Ethical Treatment of Animals). I am a vegetarian, and I protest against animals in circuses and the killing of animals for their fur and other body parts. I became a member of PETA because I do not agree with the thoughtless cruelty going on today. The lives of animals are in our hands, and we must take responsibility for them. Everybody should try to be a peacemaker of the world and end animal cruelty. "

Painful end

Traps set in the wild to catch fur-bearing animals often cause a slow and painful death. The traps are baited with food and left untended, so they attract and kill the wrong animals. Foxes, birds, and pet cats and dogs often die, as well as those intended for the fur market.

Animal products

It is hard to believe that anybody would want to buy a crocodile skull (top left). But, as with all the objects in this display, it was confiscated by customs officials from vacationers returning home. These souvenirs were the result of hunting threatened animals. If people stop buying illegal animal products, poachers will stop providing them.

The **Siamese crocodile** is **extinct** in parts of **Southeast Asia** as a result of **trade** in its **hide**

Customs seizures

Officials seized these jaguar skins as they were being smuggled out of Brazil. The CITES (Convention on International Trade in Endangered Species) treaty is a set of rules that limits the trade in animals and animal products. These rules aim to stop endangered species from being taken from one country to another and help to protect wild species. But some people still risk breaking the law if the price is right.

TIM LUFFMAN
SPECIALIST CUSTOMS OFFICER

TIM LUFFMAN WORKS AS PART OF THE CITES (CONVENTION ON THE INTERNATIONAL TRADE IN ENDANGERED SPECIES) TEAM AT HEATHROW AIRPORT, LONDON, UK. Whenever rare live animals or animal products pass through the airport, Tim is responsible for checking that they are being imported legally and in suitable conditions.

A day in the life of a
SPECIALIST CUSTOMS OFFICER

The CITES team is part of HM Customs and Excise – the organization that regulates the passage of goods into the UK.

Last chance
One-horned rhinos are endangered in the wild. Captive breeding in zoos may be their only chance of survival.

Today, Tim will be called on to examine and identify alligators and ivory, snakeskin, rhinos, and tortoises. He never knows what will arrive next, so he can never plan his day in advance.

Animal airport
Planes land at Heathrow from all parts of the world, bringing animals into the UK – legally as well as illegally.

7:00am I arrive in the office to cover the early shift. Airplanes land here day and night, so at least one member of the CITES team has to be available at all times. When animals are brought into the UK legally, we can prepare for their arrival. But we are also called to the scene when customs officers pick up something suspicious, and need us to deal with it.

Ivory elephant tusk

Fake ivory buttons

The real thing
Tim is able to tell at a glance whether an item stopped at customs is made of real or fake ivory.

7:30am My first job of the day is to check on some rare Indian rhinos, and quickly clear them through customs. These animals have been flown in from Nepal in large, airy crates, but we do not want to delay them any longer than is necessary. Traveling long distances can be stressful for wild animals, even when their transport conditions are good. I check all the paperwork that has come with the rhinos.

Everything is in order, so we allow them into the country. They head on to a breeding program at an English zoo.

8:30am I get a call to say that officers have stopped a passenger from Hong Kong who is carrying a

Animal reception center
If Tim suspects that an animal is being imported illegally, he takes it to the reception center to examine it.

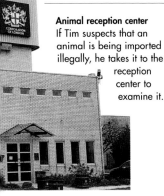

> **It is important for me to keep an open mind with everything I examine, and to try to think like a smuggler.**

Moving snakes
The sand boas, like most small reptiles, travel in bags inside wooden crates. This method of transport keeps them safe and calm.

carving that could be made from illegal ivory. I go to examine the carving and can confirm that it is made from plastic imitation ivory, and not elephant tusk. Real ivory is easy to spot because it has a criss-cross pattern that can be seen with the naked eye. The passenger is allowed to go on his way.

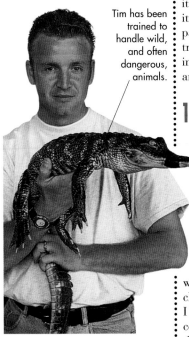

Tim has been trained to handle wild, and often dangerous, animals.

Snap shut
Tim tapes an alligator's mouth shut so that it cannot bite him, and grips its tail firmly to avoid being swiped.

9:00am Some of the animals I come across can be dangerous, and my next job is a good example of this. Twenty American alligators are waiting to be checked before they can be allowed to continue on to their destination – an English zoo. I have to lift each alligator out of its traveling crate to make sure

it is healthy. I also check that its species and size match its paperwork, because some people try to smuggle rare species using inaccurate or misleading import and export documents.

10:30am I am told that 200 snakes from Zambia have arrived at the animal reception center. The paperwork we require to inspect them has also been delivered. The invoice lists one species of snake – East African sand boas. Rob, an expert in the identification and handling of snakes, inspects the boas with me. They are packed in cloth bags inside wooden boxes. I have to remove each snake to count them. Rob and I conclude that the snakes are the right species, but we are not happy with the paperwork. I check in some reference books, and find that this species of snake is not actually found in Zambia. I suspect these ones have been taken from a country that bans their export and then smuggled into Zambia. This makes all the paperwork illegal. The snakes were destined for pet stores in the US, but I arrange to send them on to zoos and specialist keepers in the UK.

12:00pm As I am eating my lunch, I am called out to the airport's mail depot. When I arrive, I am presented with a snakeskin handbag. I instantly recognize the skin as that of a reticulated python. It requires CITES paperwork to enter the country legally. In this case, the passenger has the right documents. Reticulated pythons are not rare, but because they are often used to make shoes and bags, they are protected. A limit of 100,000 of the snakes are allowed to be exported from their country of origin each year.

2:00pm I receive a phone call from a member of the public. The caller has seen some exotic tortoises for sale in a local pet store, and is concerned that they may have been smuggled into the country. I assure the person that there is a legal trade in many exotic animals, but I decide to ask the local customs office in that area to investigate. Just when I am about to go home for the day, I receive a phone call from the local customs office. The animals spotted in the pet store were in fact Asian brown tortoises, and they had been legally brought into the UK for sale as pets. It is illegal to import rarer species of tortoise, but even these can be bred in this country to be sold as pets.

3:15pm Before leaving to go home, I update the late team on the day's events. I wonder what the rest of the day will bring my colleagues.

Tortoise trade
Providing that Asian brown tortoises are transported in reasonable conditions, and have the right paperwork, it is legal to import them into the UK.

This tortoise has traveled on a bed of shredded paper to keep it warm and comfortable.

Many countries now have laws controlling trade in rare and exotic animals

PET *trade*

Popularity can be dangerous

for wild animals. Lots of people like to keep exotic or foreign creatures as pets or for collections, but the trade has helped bring about the decline of some wildlife species. High-value rare animals are snatched from the wild, smuggled long distances in cramped containers, and sold illegally through pet shops and dealers. Strict laws and undercover investigations are two ways to regulate the trade. Another is for people who buy the animals to make sure that they come from approved sources.

Operation Chameleon, an investigation in the US, has stopped many **reptile smugglers** from trading

Red-kneed tarantula
These Mexican spiders make interesting pets, but wild populations are declining due to the pet trade.

Animal trappers
Red-kneed tarantulas and gouldian finches are two species of animals harmed by the pet trade. The rarer a species gets, the more demand there is for it. Trappers steal young birds from their nests and dig out spiders like tarantulas from their burrows.

Cage birds
Gouldian finches have declined in the wild in Australia partly because large numbers of them have been trapped for sale as pets.

Squashed snakes
Burmese pythons are sometimes transported hidden in suitcases. Hundreds of young snakes may be squashed into one bag.

Smuggled victims

These blue-and-yellow macaws, smuggled from South America, are being kept in cramped conditions. On average, four parrots die for every one that reaches its destination, because of cruel capture and transport methods. Smuggled birds are often packed in hidden containers without sufficient space or air.

Difficult pets

Reptiles, such as this Burmese python, are shipped across the world to live in conditions totally different from their tropical homes. To stay healthy, reptiles need special light to simulate sunlight, warm temperature conditions, and the right food. Many owners find exotic pets too demanding and neglect or abandon them.

Swallowtail birdwing butterfly

Queen Alexandra birdwing butterfly

At least 58 species of parrot are at risk as a direct result of the pet trade

Reared for market

Villagers in Papua New Guinea have set up caterpillar gardens and hatching cages to raise large numbers of spectacular birdwing butterflies for export to collectors. Breeding in captivity satisfies the demand for exotic animals without plundering wild populations.

Saved in time

The Sepilok Rehabilitation Center in Borneo cares for orangutans that have been confiscated from smugglers. They are looked after until they are ready for release back into their forest home. Efforts to return these orangutans to the wild are not easy. The rescued animals are often in poor health, stressed, and far from their original habitat.

ACTION!
CARE FOR PETS

Keep pets that you can care for properly – tropical animals need special conditions and may live for a long time.

Write to a group that campaigns against illegal trade in exotic pets, and see if you can help.

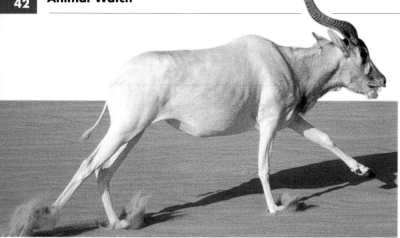

Hunted down

After years of being hunted for sport and for their prized horns, less than 200 addax still roam the deserts of North Africa. Although they are swift runners, they cannot easily escape when chased across the sands by hunters in vehicles. These, and many other hoofed animals of the open country, are still at risk from hunting.

Safari hunters will pay $10,000 for a license to shoot one elephant

Hunting controls can make the difference between survival and extinction for threatened animals

Hunting *for sport*

Safari income

The hunter who shot this Cape buffalo in Zimbabwe did so legally. Some southern African countries allow hunting in reserves because it can benefit conservation. Tourists pay for these animal trophies. Some of the money is then put back into the reserve to fund the upkeep of the land and its animal inhabitants.

Wild animals have been hunted for the thrill of the sport since ancient times. Today, all sorts of people go shooting or fishing for fun. Hunting as a hobby does not always damage wildlife populations, but some people think it is wrong to kill an animal for amusement. Careless or excessive hunting can be cruel to animals, and can push rare species closer to extinction. Some conservationists argue that controlled hunting in reserves and private parks can help to protect natural habitats, and even the species that are hunted there – the species are better protected because the hunting brings in money.

"I live in Treviso in Italy. From my bedroom window I can see and hear many birds – small ones like robins, woodpeckers, and pigeons, but also big ones like woodcocks and pheasants. A few kilometers from my house is a place where storks nest during their migration. In the breeding season I hear hunters shooting and see them with their rifles and dogs. I hope all the birds find shelter in my yard and that the hunters find nothing. I like birds because they are free to fly in the sky. Maybe one day the hunting will be banned, and there will be even more birds around my house."

Alessandro Carboni

Hazardous journey

Honey buzzards are a target for hunters in Italy and Malta as they migrate between Europe and Africa. They are among the millions of birds shot out of the skies every year as they fly across the Mediterranean region. Conservation groups in many countries now campaign against this seasonal slaughter.

About **100,000** birds of prey **are shot** in Malta every year

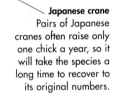

Japanese crane
Pairs of Japanese cranes often raise only one chick a year, so it will take the species a long time to recover to its original numbers.

Success story

In the 1920s, European visitors to Japan hunted the Japanese crane close to extinction. Only 20 of the birds were left. The crane was then given protection from the hunters, and its numbers have now risen to about 600. Changes in people's attitudes play an important part in the race to save rare animals from extinction through overhunting.

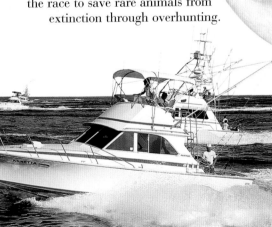

Fishing for fun

Fishing is big business in places like Hawaii. Although angling is one of the most accepted forms of hunting, it can reduce fish populations if people do not follow the rules. Laws protect rare species of fish, such as the striped bass, Nassau grouper, and sturgeon.

BACK FROM
THE BRINK

MORE PEOPLE THAN EVER ARE NOW TAKING ACTION TO PRESERVE HABITATS. THEY ARE ALSO TRYING TO HELP THREATENED wildlife and rescue species that are in danger of extinction. Today, many conservation projects are in progress around the world, dedicated to protecting and restoring wildlife populations.

Gray wolves (main picture) are now starting to make a comeback in some regions where they had declined drastically. They have been helped by conservation measures such as hunting laws, habitat protection, and the reintroduction of captive-bred wolves into the wild. Actions like these can stop more species from suffering the fate of the golden toad (inset), which recently became extinct.

“There is still time to save species and ecosystems – our failure to do so will not be forgiven by future generations.”

WORLD COMMISSION ON ENVIRONMENT AND DEVELOPMENT, 1987

The Red List

The World Conservation Union's Red List names threatened animal species, such as the Malayan tapir, the douc langur, and the Chinese alligator. Animals at immediate risk of dying out are classified as "critically endangered," those that may be extinct in the near future are listed as "endangered," and those at risk in the longer term are "vulnerable."

Vulnerable tapir
Habitat loss has reduced wild populations of Malayan tapirs to a few isolated groups.

Endangered monkey
In its forest home in Laos and Vietnam, the douc langur has been hunted close to extinction.

Critically endangered alligator
Habitat destruction has made the Chinese alligator the rarest of the crocodile relatives.

Krill are the main food in the diet of five species of whales.

Trawlers remove hundreds of thousands of tons of krill from the seas every year.

MONITOR
and research

Finding out

Krill are small crustaceans that are harvested from the Antarctic seas in huge quantities to be sold as food for farm animals. We do not know how this will affect wild animals, such as the whales, seals, and penguins that depend on krill for food. More research is needed to fill the gaps in our knowledge of marine life.

Accurate information is vital in the battle to save the world's wildlife. The research and monitoring work carried out by scientists provides the building blocks for successful conservation. Monitoring tells us which animals are in most danger, how large their populations are, and why they are under threat. Researchers find out what animals eat, where they find their food, and how they live and breed. This research shows us how to care for animals in captivity and what we can do to conserve them. Armed with this knowledge, we can launch campaigns and design projects to protect animals and their habitats.

Research techniques

This snow leopard is fitted with a collar that contains a radio transmitter. This allows researchers to keep track of its movements in the mountains of Kashmir. Research techniques like this are useful for studying animals that are hard to observe in their natural environment.

"Without information we are working in the dark."

THE WILDLIFE PRESERVATION TRUST INTERNATIONAL

Scientists around the world gather the information that is used to compile the Red List

Venom can be collected from the fangs without harming the snake.

The Gaboon viper injects venom into its prey through its fangs.

Snake bite

Venom from poisonous animals, such as vipers, can be used to make medicines that prevent blood clots or act as painkillers. The snakes can be reared in captivity and "milked" for their venom. The more we learn about animals through research, the more we can benefit without harming them.

Captive care

Seahorses are reared in experimental ponds in Vietnam to improve techniques in breeding them for sale. Successful breeding, or aquaculture, of seahorses in captivity could take the pressure off wild populations, which are being reduced along many coasts and reefs off Southeast Asia.

EXPERIMENT

SNAIL MONITOR

You will need: flowerpot, large garden snails, small can of nontoxic paint*, paintbrush, protective gloves.

1 PUT A LARGE CLAY FLOWERPOT upside down in a damp part of a yard, leaving one edge propped up so that snails can get in and out.

2 GO BACK TO THE FLOWERPOT THE NEXT DAY, and collect any snails that are inside. Paint a number on each snail, then put them back in the flowerpot.

Nontoxic paint will not harm the snail or the environment.

3 CHECK THE FLOWERPOT EACH DAY. Write down which marked snails return to your pot, and paint numbers on any new arrivals. You may find that the same snails rest in your pot over and over again.

This shows that: you can learn how snails behave by tracking a sample group. Information like this helps conservationists protect wildlife.

*Check that paint is water-based, nonsolvent, and environmentally friendly.

KOALA RESCUE EXPERT
AUDREY KOOSMEN

AUDREY KOOSMEN HAS A LICENSE FROM THE NATIONAL PARKS AND WILDLIFE SERVICE THAT PERMITS HER TO TAKE IN ANIMALS THAT NEED HELP. Snowflake (left) is one of more than 300 sick, injured, and orphaned koalas that Audrey has cared for from her home in Blackalls Park, Newcastle, Australia.

A day in the life of a
KOALA RESCUE EXPERT

Rescuing koalas takes a lot of time and effort, but the work Audrey does helps to conserve a unique Australian marsupial species.

Today, Audrey has three koalas to care for – Little Al, Dimples, and Cinders. She rescued her first native animal when she was 16 and now teaches students the skills she has learned.

6:00am The alarm clock rings and my day begins. Little Al, an orphaned baby koala, known as a joey, is already awake in his basket beside my bed. His mother was killed by a car, and he was rescued from her pouch. Because

Koala country
Audrey lives near areas of wild trees and plants known as the bush. The bush of New South Wales is home to more koalas than anywhere else. Some of Audrey's patients are victims of natural bush fires, but others are caught in fires set by people.

Pouch protection
Audrey keeps Little Al in a specially made cloth pouch, which keeps him warm and safe, as if he were in his mother's pouch. Koalas do not usually begin to leave their mother's pouch until they are about seven months old.

he is only six months old, he needs round-the-clock care and has to be fed a special, warmed milk formula from a bottle. First of all, I gently take him out of his pouch and encourage him to

produce droppings on some newspaper. This means his pouch will stay clean. He drinks his milk and then goes straight back to sleep. Even adult koalas rest for up to 20 hours each day – they need to save as much energy as possible because their diet of eucalyptus does not give them much energy.

7:00am By the time I have fed Little Al, Dimples is awake. He is a nine-year-old koala, and was brought to me with a nasty eye infection, which is common in koalas. I keep Dimples in a cage I made

from a wooden baby's crib. He has blankets and pillows around him to keep him cozy. I bathe his eyes with warm water and apply eye cream. He is very naughty when having his eyes bathed – he does not like it at all. Afterwards I give him a drink of milk formula, which cheers him up. Dimples was underweight when he came to me, so he has a more concentrated mix of the milk formula I usually give to joeys, to build him up and encourage him to eat. I also give him some fresh eucalyptus leaves. He feeds for an hour before falling asleep.

Special care
Sick koalas like Dimples need to be kept warm and comfortable, and have to be watched closely. Such intensive care also allows Audrey to learn about the needs of the animals in her care.

8:30am Outside, Cinders is waiting for her fresh leaves. She was badly burned on her ears, paws, nose, and back in a bush fire. I gave her lots of fluids, 24-hour care, and gentle stretching exercises to keep her muscles working while she was very ill. She is well enough now to live in the aviary in the garden. I pick up the dirty newspaper that I placed on the aviary floor to catch her pellets, or droppings. I have to count them, as this tells me how much she is eating. I give

Finding fresh food
On some days, students follow Audrey as she works, learning which leaves to pick, where to find them, and how many to take.

Mother figure
When a baby koala loses its mother, it may cry for days, making a sound like a human baby. Little Al is comforted by his teddy bear

Cinders three different species of eucalyptus leaves, because koalas eat a variety in the wild. She begins to feed right away. I pat her and scratch under her chin, which she loves.

10:00am Little Al is awake again, and ready for his bottle. I play with him and his teddy bear for 15 minutes. He then drinks his milk and drops off to sleep – again!

11:00am Captive koalas make a lot of laundry and waste. But, once I've done the laundry and put the old leaves on the compost heap, I can go out in the bush leaf collecting. Koalas are fussy and enjoy only the freshest leaves. I store the new eucalyptus in containers of clean water and keep it cool.

These young leaves are smaller and more rounded than older eucalyptus leaves.

66 The biggest thrill I get is when a koala I have cared for is released, and then I see it roaming free again. **99**

1:00pm I have just finished the next round of feeding and treatments when the vet stops by. He visits me three times a week to see how all the koalas are doing. He examines Cinders first. She does not like being woken up and becomes very cranky and tries to bite him. The vet attaches a bright yellow ear tag and a radio collar so that she can be recognized, tracked, and checked when she is released next week. Dimples is seen next, and the vet is very happy with his eyes. Last of all, Little Al is woken for his check, and the vet assures me that he has put on a healthy amount of weight. In a few months, he will be big enough to survive in the wild.

4:30pm I spend some time with Cinders when I go to give her the last meal of the day. She is very special to me as I have been caring for her for 11 months. I can tell she is ready for release because she looks fit and strong. I will miss her when she is returned to the wild, but will be happy to see

Cinders will soon get used to wearing a radio collar.

Practice makes perfect
Cinders is a mature koala, but she has been in captivity a long time. She needs to practice climbing and get fit before she is returned to the wild.

her free again. The bush is a dangerous place, especially in the breeding season. At this time koalas wander further afield, crossing roads and coming into contact with people and predators, but I know it is where she belongs.

6:00pm Dimples is calling – he must be hungry. I bathe his eyes again, then give him some milk. I hand-feed him some of his favorite eucalyptus flowers. He will soon be well enough to live in the aviary – one step away from freedom.

7:30pm In my bedroom, Little Al is awake, and he decides to get out of his pouch to look around. I have a heater going in the room all the time to keep him very warm. He nibbles on some soft, young leaves, then drinks only half of his milk before he falls asleep.

9:00pm After a final check on Cinders and Dimples, I too go off to bed. In just three hours time I will have to get up to feed Little Al again.

RUN WILD
RUN FREE

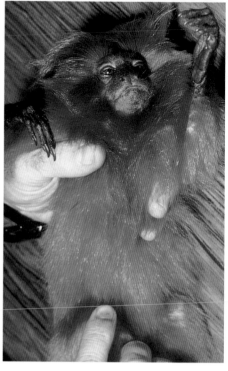

Some animal species face such difficulties and dangers that they need help now if they are to continue to live in the wild in the future. Conservationists have set up programs to breed many of these vulnerable animals in captivity. Their goal is to make sure that, whatever happens in the wild, the species does not die out completely. When enough of the animals have been raised in captivity, and when their chances of survival in their natural homes have improved, they can be released, or reintroduced, into the wild.

Breeding success

Almost all of the golden lion tamarin's forest habitat in southeastern Brazil has been destroyed to clear the land for farming. A worldwide captive-breeding project was launched in the 1980s to save the monkey from extinction. After 10 years, more than 500 tamarins had been raised in captivity, and some are now being returned to freedom.

Tuataras are now being released on islands off the coast of New Zealand.

ACTION!
SAVE SPECIES

Find out if there is a zoo near your home that has a captive-breeding program and ask if your school can organize a trip there.

Always put wild creatures back where you found them if you remove them for study.

Helping hand
Captive female tuataras are given chemicals, called hormones, to help them produce more young than they would in the wild.

Intensive care

In captivity, animals are safe from predators and poachers, but many need special care if they are to stay healthy and eventually breed. Some animals born in captivity have to be given foster parents. Others are hand-reared, which means they need to be bottle-fed at regular intervals.

Million-dollar ferrets
Black-footed ferrets are now being returned to the wild in the US, following an expensive captive-breeding program.

Costs of captivity

The number of Sumatran rhinoceroses in the wild became so small that 38 of about 120 remaining animals were taken from the wild for captive breeding. But almost all the captives failed to produce calves. Because it is so expensive and does not always work, captive breeding should be used only as a last resort.

The European bison thrives once again in the wild.

"Captive breeding and reintroduction require long-term effort."

JOHN MARZLUFF
PROFESSOR OF WILDLIFE SCIENCE

Back in the wild

Once extinct in the wild, mainly as a result of habitat loss, the European bison made its return in 1956. Captive-bred animals were released into a protected forest in Poland, where their numbers are steadily increasing. The herds of European bison are carefully monitored, which is important if the reintroduced animals are to do well.

Persistent problems

The reintroduction of the Arabian oryx to its desert home has been one of the great conservation successes of recent years. But, as the thriving wild herd grew to 400, poachers returned recently to capture live animals for private collectors. Reintroducing captive-bred animals to the wild works only if the threats they once faced have disappeared.

A safer start in life

Kemp's ridley turtles live in the Pacific Ocean and the Gulf of Mexico. They normally lose most of their eggs and young to predators and poachers, so conservationists are giving them a head start. The turtles' eggs are collected from the wild and put in hatcheries until the young are big enough to survive on their own.

Parks and RESERVES

All shapes and sizes

Yosemite National Park in California is home to rare animals, such as the puma, the black bear, and the great gray owl. Yosemite covers 1,864 sq miles (3,000 sq km), but smaller pond, woodland, and meadow reserves are just as important.

National parks, nature reserves, and other protected places are areas of land, or sometimes sea, that are set aside for nature conservation. They are important refuges for wildlife. Park staff work hard to protect the environment and the animals that live there. Because parks and reserves preserve whole habitats, they benefit a range of different species. But these areas are not always popular with local people because they may stop them from using the land for their own needs.

ACTION!
SAVE HABITATS

Visit a nature reserve and see if you can join volunteers who are helping with conservation work.

Find out more about organizations that support wild animal reserves.

Elephant trouble

National parks have played an important role in conserving African elephants. In some parks, elephant herds have become so large that they have begun to damage the parks' vegetation. Occasionally, staff have to shoot, or cull, some animals to reduce numbers and prevent overcrowding.

Success story

Parks set up in the Andes Mountains, South America, have helped to save the vicuña, a relative of the camel. In 1965, only 6,000 vicuñas remained, due to hunting for their fleece. Now safe from poachers, their numbers have risen to almost 100,000.

Parks and people

This tourist guide in a reserve in Madagascar is tempting a ring-tailed lemur into the open for visitors. Protected areas like this can provide jobs in tourism for local people who can no longer hunt or clear land for farming to make a living. Conservationists are trying to find more ways to ease the hardship that parks can cause for local communities.

Animal guards
Some ex-poachers now work as guards so that they can make a living without hunting protected animals.

There are almost **50,000** animal **parks** and **reserves** in the **world**

❝ I live in Cape Town in South Africa, and last week I visited Pilanesburg National Park. We saw impala, wildebeest, birds, and springbok. Then, right in front of us was an elephant. He had no idea we were watching him eat and knock down trees! That huge gray animal will stay in my mind forever. Last of all, we saw hippos. Using binoculars we could watch them playing in the water. I had a terrific day at Pilanesburg, and I think we should work together to protect these animals so that people in the future can enjoy seeing them too. ❞ Maya Schkolne

Park life
Most African elephants now live in national parks like the Serengeti in Tanzania.

Extreme measures

Armed guards, like this one from Kenya, patrol some parks to protect animals from people who enter illegally to hunt or poach wildlife. Such drastic measures show how serious the clash between conservation and people can be. In some places, whole villages have been moved to make way for parks, causing resentment among local people.

The **Pulau Ubin** reserve in Singapore has **saved** the native **fruit bat** from **extinction**

RARE ANIMAL KEEPER
MICHELLE JAMISON

MICHELLE JAMISON'S DAYS ARE DEDICATED TO CARING FOR RARE MAMMALS AT THE PHILADELPHIA ZOO. WHEN SHE IS NOT FEEDING THE ANIMALS, cleaning their enclosures, or giving them things to play with, she talks to visitors, answering their questions about the animals and teaching them about conservation.

Natural look
There are plenty of trees and green spaces at the zoo, to create a natural environment for animals and visitors.

A day in the life of a
RARE ANIMAL KEEPER

Keeping rare animals in zoos can help to raise funds for their conservation in the wild.

Zoos working together
Philadelphia Zoo is located in Pennsylvania and takes part in breeding programs with zoos all over the US.

Today, Michelle has to see to the different needs of the species in her care. It takes a great deal of work to keep captive animals well and happy.

7:30am The morning starts with a meeting of vets and keepers, to discuss events from the previous day. We update each other on any animal births or deaths, and on other zoo activities. Today, I hear that a rare Amur leopard cub has been born in the zoo's lion house. Keepers there are monitoring the cub through a hidden camera in the mother's den.

8:00am It is time for me to check on the animals in my care. I am responsible for two red pandas (Sparkler and his son Maudin), two male giant otters (Banjo and Rio), two snow leopards (Du, a female, and Athos, a male), and three coatis, a type of South American raccoon, (Ira and Izzy, both males, and Myra, a female).

Protective gloves

Trout

Mountain home
Snow leopards live wild only in the mountains of central Asia.

Coatis have strong paws and long snouts, to help them forage for fruit and insects in the wild.

8:30am I prepare the animal exhibits by cleaning and refilling the water bowls and adding enrichment items. These are things to entertain the animals and stop them from becoming bored. Wild animals spend all their time searching for food, mates, and a place to live. In zoos all this is provided, so it is important to keep them active and busy in other ways. For the coatis, I fill bags with hay and hide raisins or crickets inside for them to find. The snow leopards love to tear apart phone books and scratch at logs, on which we've dribbled catnip or fish oil scent. Rubber toys and balls occupy the otters, and the young red panda plays for hours with a ball in his exhibit. The red pandas also like to chew bamboo and fruit-scented wood.

leopards in North American zoos are part of this plan. The SSP coordinator knows how all of them are related, and he makes decisions about which snow leopards should breed. This ensures that zoos do not breed close relatives or produce more cubs than there is room for in captivity. Our snow leopards do not have a breeding recommendation at the moment, but conservation in zoos is not just about breeding. Housing non-breeding cats is an important part of the SSP's management of the species.

10:30am I give the otters their first meal – they have one trout each, with vitamins hidden in the gills. Wild South American giant otters eat mainly fish, but they are also known to attack large snakes and other reptiles. Giant otters have extremely sharp teeth for tackling their prey, so I wear thick gloves to protect myself when I feed them.

12:00pm I encourage our coatis to make an appearance for the public. But the temperature outside is not to their satisfaction, and they cling to the hammocks in their heated den and will not venture out. The climate in their South American home is warm all year round, and they do not appreciate chilly Philadelphia days. I then put the giant otters on exhibit. They are the most valuable, endangered animals in my care, and are very sensitive to changes in their water. Water pollution in the wild, along with overhunting for their fur, is responsible for them now being so rare, so I make sure the quality of their water is perfect. I also give the otters a second meal – more fish, of course. Feeding little and often helps to prevent captive animals from becoming restless. While I feed the giant otters, I am videotaped

The high life
With their long, flexible tails and strong legs, coatis are built to climb. Their enclosure has plenty of trees and branches.

66 Captive breeding and increased public awareness are necessary to save endangered animals and their vanishing habitats. **99**

for an educational video the zoo is making. The video will link students to zoo and conservation projects via the internet. After the otters, it is the red pandas' turn to be fed. I give them fresh bamboo, their favorite food in the wild, and a vitamin-rich mix to keep them in top condition.

1:00pm I switch the snow leopards around so that the female, Du, can go in the outdoor enclosure for some fresh air, exercise, and a change of scenery.

3:00pm I clean the animals' indoor shelters and add enrichment items to occupy them overnight. I then bring the animals in, taking care not to release an animal or put it in the wrong shelter. I give the snow leopards

a meal of horse or chicken meat in their den, then check all the locks twice, making sure the warning signs on the enclosures say "exhibit empty."

5:30pm Finally, I prepare my keeper report to be reviewed at tomorrow's meeting. The discussions help us to understand the needs of these rare animals.

Feeding fun
Michelle turns feeding time into a game for the red pandas, to entertain them.

Life story
Keeping giant otters in captivity allows the zoo to tell visitors the story of their struggle in the wild, and to get support for their protection.

9:00am My next job is to put the male snow leopard on exhibit for the first half of the day. He and the female do not get along so they have to swap time on exhibit. Du and Athos can see, hear, and smell each other through a door in their dens so we hope that they will eventually become friends. Our snow leopards are part of the snow leopard Species Survival Plan (SSP). Most snow

ZOO DEBATE

Panda controversy

People disagree about whether giant pandas should be kept in zoos. They are popular exhibits, but in the past, have been taken from the wild to satisfy zoos' demands. The species is now under threat of extinction, and breeding in zoos may save it. However, it is difficult to breed giant pandas in captivity.

Zoos containing wild animals have been around since ancient times, and today there are more than 10,000 zoos throughout the world. For many years, animal lovers and conservationists have campaigned to improve the conditions in which animals are kept. They have helped to bring about important changes at many zoos, but there are still lots of places where animals are kept in terrible conditions. Today, there is heated debate about what the proper role of zoos should be, and some people believe that keeping animals in zoos of any kind is wrong.

ACTION!
IMPROVE ZOOS

Contact a group campaigning to improve conditions for animals in zoos and find out about their work.

Adopt a zoo animal – you will help pay for its care and also learn about the animal.

At least **20 animal** species owe their **survival** to conservation in zoos

New zoos

Many modern zoos provide natural, spacious enclosures for their animals, with trees to climb and places to hide. Large creatures, such as rhinos, can live in groups and behave much as they would in the wild. Until recently, home to most zoo animals was a bare cage with a concrete floor and metal bars.

Roaming rhinos
Rhinoceroses are able to roam in the spacious, semi-natural enclosures at San Diego Wild Animal Park in California.

Amusement or education

At one time, zoos used to dress chimpanzees in clothes and make them perform to amuse visitors. Today, more and more zoos are trying to educate people about wildlife instead of just entertaining them. They show visitors how animals behave naturally and provide information about conservation.

"Our own future lies in the preservation of other creatures."

ZOOCHECK

Saved by zoos

Przewalski's wild horse is an ancestor of the domestic horse. It would have died out long ago if herds had not been preserved in zoos in Eurasia and North America. The species became extinct in the wild in 1968, but a captive herd had been established several decades earlier. The species has since survived in zoos through 14 generations, and some horses have been released into the wild in parts of Eastern Europe. The total population today is about 2,000.

WOODLOUSE WORLD — EXPERIMENT

You will need: an old shoe box, scissors, protective gloves, damp leaves and soil, cotton, about ten woodlice – you will find them outside under stones, plant-pots, and dead leaves.

1 CUT THE LID OF THE shoe box in half. Place a pile of damp leaves and soil at one end of the box and some dry cotton at the other end.

2 GENTLY RELEASE the woodlice into the middle of the box. Put one half of the lid on the box above the leaves and soil.

3 PLACE THE BOX in a bright place and watch the woodlice. They should all go to the dark and damp end of the box and ignore the dry cotton at the light end of the box.

Within seconds, the woodlice decide which way to go.

This shows that: animals are happiest in conditions that are most like their natural habitat. Woodlice like damp and dark places and are not happy in light and dry conditions. Remember to put the woodlice back outside when the experiment is over.

Zoos to the rescue

The California condor almost became extinct in the wild as a result of egg-collecting and pesticide poisoning, but it now flies free again. Its return is thanks to zoos in San Diego and Los Angeles, which bred birds in captivity for release into the wild. Zoos worldwide play an important part in the conservation of species.

Action Plan

IF YOU CARE ABOUT THE PLANET and want to help save the wildlife that shares it with you, there are lots of organizations that will help you to get involved. This list includes some US and international organizations that you can write to or visit on the internet.

American Society for the Prevention of Cruelty to Animals (ASPCA)
A national charity involved in all aspects of animal welfare.

www.aspca.org

424 East 92nd St
New York, NY 10128

American Zoo and Aquarium Association (AZA)
Look up your local zoo or aquarium and find out how endangered species are being helped.

www.aza.org

8403 Colesville Road
Suite 710
Silver Spring, MD 20910

British Butterfly Conservation Society
A society dedicated to conserving butterflies and their habitats.

PO Box 222
Dedham
Colchester
Essex CO7 6EY
UK

Canadian Wildlife Federation
The CWF is dedicated to fostering awareness and protection of Canada's wildlife, as well as promoting sustainable use of national resources.

www.cwf-fcf.org

350 Michael Cowpland Drive
Kanata, ON K2M 2W1
Canada

Care for the Wild
A wildlife charity that protects animals from cruelty and exploitation. Also supports work to help endangered species worldwide.

www.careforthewild.org

PO Box 46250
Madison, WI 53744-6250

Environmental Investigation Agency (EIA)
An international campaigning organization committed to improving conservation laws – and making sure

that existing laws are upheld. EIA agents work worldwide, often undercover.

www.eia-international.org

PO Box 53343
Washington, DC 20009

Fabulous Kakapo
The website for this New Zealand-based charity is full of information about the race to save the kakapo from the brink of extinction.

www.kakapo.net

Recovery Programme
PO Box 10-420
Wellington
New Zealand

Friends of the Earth
An international network of environmental groups that commissions research and campaigns for changes in the law.

www.foe.org

1025 Vermont Ave, NW
3rd Floor
Washington, DC 20005-6303

Greenpeace
One of the world's main environmental organizations, involved in direct action to safeguard the planet's future.

www.greenpeace.org

702 H Street NW
Washington, DC 20001

Humane Society of Canada
This Canadian organization campaigns for the protection of animals and the environment and promotes alternatives to the use of animals in research.

www.humanesociety.com

347 Bay Street, Suite 806
Toronto, ON M5H 2R7
Canada

International Rhino Foundation
A charity providing funding to help rhinos in the wild and in captivity.

www.rhinos-irf.org

14000 International Road
Cumberland
Ohio 43732

International Union for the Conservation of Nature and Natural Resources (IUCN)
The world's largest conservation-related organization that brings together 76 states and many other groups in a unique worldwide partnership.

www.iucn.org

Rue Mauverney 28
CH-1196 Gland
Switzerland

Orangutan Foundation International
Adopt an orangutan through this charity and help to fund conservation of the animal's rainforest home.

www.orangutan.org

822 S. Wellesley Avenue
Los Angeles, CA 90049

People for the Ethical Treatment of Animals (PETA)
This group campaigns to prevent animal cruelty and abuse worldwide.

www.peta-online.org

501 Front Street
Norfolk, VA 23510

Rain Forest Action Network
This organization's website has lots of ideas for things you can do to help save the world's rain forests.

www.ran.org

221 Pine Street
Suite 500
San Francisco, CA 94104

San Diego Zoo Wild Animal Park
Animal enclosures in this internationally famous zoo are designed to resemble animals' natural habitats as closely as possible. San Diego Zoo also takes part in rare species breeding programmes.

www.sandiegozoo.org

15500 San Pasqual Valley Road
Escondido, CA 92027-7017

Sierra Club of Canada
This international organization campaigns to protect wildlife, wilderness, and unspoiled habitats.

www.sierraclub.ca

412-1 Nicholas Street
Ottawa, ON K1N 7B7
Canada

TRAFFIC International
The wildlife trade monitoring program of the WWF and the IUCN. TRAFFIC works to enforce laws that restrict the trade in live rare animals for the pet trade and animal parts for fashion and medicine.

www.traffic.org

1250 24th St, NW
Washington, DC 20037

United States Fish and Wildlife Service
Helps protect a healthy environment for fish, wildlife, and people. Main interests are migratory birds, endangered species, marine mammals, freshwater and migratory fish.

www.fws.gov

Department of the Interior
1849 C Street NW
Washington, DC 20240

Whale and Dolphin Conservation Society
A charity that campaigns for protection of whales, dolphins, and porpoises.

www.wdcs.org

Alexander House
James St. West
Bath BA1 2BT
UK

Wildlife Protection Society of India
This organization campaigns against the illegal trade in tigers and other wildlife.

www.nbs.it/tiger

Thapar House
124 Janpath
New Delhi 110001
India

World Conservation Monitoring Centre (WCMC)
This organization collects and publishes information about endangered species, as well as environmental issues.

www.wcmc.org.uk

219 Huntingdon Road
Cambridge CB3 0DL
UK

Worldwide Fund for Nature (WWF)
The world's largest conservation organization. Visit the website to find out what the WWF does and to check out the Living Planet Report.

www.panda.org

1250 24th St NW
Washington, DC 20037-1175

Zoocheck
A charity protecting animals in captivity through education and campaigning.

www.zoocheck.com

3266 Yonge Street
Suite 1417
Toronto ON M4N 3P6
Canada

Index

Credits

Dorling Kindersley would like to thank:
Hettie Gets at WWF South Africa; Lynn Bresler for the index.

Steve Gorton for photography of the experiments, and hand model Emily Gorton.

Special thanks to Day in the Life experts and their organizations – Michael Mitchell (Wetlands Manager); Andrew Routh (Wildlife Vet); Tim Luffman (Specialist Customs Officer); Audrey Koosmen (Koala Rescue Expert); Michelle Jamison (Rare Species Keeper).

Additional photography: Jane Burton, Andy Crawford, Philip Dowell, Frank Greenaway, Colin Keates, Dave King, Liz McAulay, Roger Phillips, Karl Shore, Harry Taylor, Kim Taylor, Jerry Young.

Picture Credits
The publishers would like to thank the following for their kind permission to reproduce the photographs:
a = above; c = center; b = below; l = left; r = right; t = top

Ardea London Ltd: Joanna Van Gruisen 46bl; Kenneth W. Fink 57br; M. Watson 13t; Nick Gordon 14tc; P. Morris 15ca; S. Roberts 12br. **Maria Bellano:** 54cra, 54–55c, 54–55tl, 55br. **Bruce Coleman Ltd:** Allan G. Potts 20bl; Andrew Davies 20–21; Dennis Green 15cl; Dr Eckart Pott 23t; Erwin & Peggy Bauer 14cl; Gerald S. Cubitt 29b; Jane Burton 47cl; Joe McDonald 29tr, 47tr; John Cancalosi 36–37; Luiz Claudio Margot 30–31, 37br, 11br; Nigel Blake 35c; Pacific Stock 43bl; Robert Maier 53bl; Rod Williams 32b, 46tcr; Steven C. Kaufman 37tr, 43cr. **Ecoscene:** Anthony Cooper 56–57b. **Environmental Images:** David Sims 23bl. **Hutchison Library:** 50tl; Bernard Regent – DIAF 51t. **International Confederation for Conservation Education:** Joe Blossom 46tr; S. Yorath 53tl; Sylvia Yoratu 46tc. **Maria Bellano:** 54tl. **Audrey Koosmen:** 48tl, 48bl, 48–49, 49tr, 49cl, 49b. **FLPA – Images of Nature:** J. Van Arkel/Foto Natura 19c. **Michael Mitchell:** 16tl, 16bl, 16br, 1617 t, 17tr, 17b. **The Natural History Museum, London:** 46cl; Colin Keates 52bl. **N.H.P.A.:** Daryl Balfour 6tl, 10–11; David Woodfall 22–23; John Shaw 53br; M. Watson 13bc; Martin Harvey 29tl; Martin Wendler 20cl, 55tr; Nigel J. Dennis 26tr; Roger Tidman 18–19t; Roy Waller 27ca; Stephen Krasemann 26bl. **Oxford Scientific Films:** Breck P. Kent 15br; David M. Dennis 33cl; David Tipling 13bl; Ian West 18–19b; Konrad Wothe 41b; Mark Hamblin 53tr; Martyn Chillmaid 40br; Michael Fogden 45cr; 18c; Paul Franklin 19tr; Richard Packwood 50–51c; Rob Cousins 50b; Stefan Meyers/Okapia 43tr; Steve Turner 51l; Tony Martin 33tl. **Planet Earth Pictures:** Alain Dragesco 42tl; Anup Shah 6–7t, 21r, 30; Brendan Ryan 42bl; Claus Meyer 14bc; David Kjaer 33b, 58–59; Franz Camenzind 22br; J. B. Duncan 34–35; K. & K. Ammann 32tr; Martin Rugner 7tr, 4445; Nigel Tucker 57cl; Steve Hopkin 22br; Tom Brakefield 54b; Yva Momatik & John Eastcott 23tr. **Andrew Routh:** 24tl, 24cr, 24bl, 24–25t, 25tc, 25br, 25cbr. **Science Photo Library:** Eye of Science 27tc. **Still Pictures:** Alberto Garcia/Christian Aid 35cr; Edward Parker 21bl, 34cr; Fredy Mercay 21cl; Jim Olive 22cl; Kevin Schafer 2–3 Endpapers, 62–63; Lynn Funkhouser 35tl; Michael Gunther 29cr, 41tr; Roland Seitre 52tr; Thomas D. Mangelsen 26–27b.

Jacket Credits
Ardea London Ltd: M Watson front inside flap. **Bruce Coleman Ltd:** Dennis Green back bl; Erwin & Peggy Bauer back tl; Joe McDonald back tr; Louie Claudio Margot front br. **N.H.P.A.:** Daryl Balfour front bc. **Planet Earth Pictures:** David Kjaer back c; K & K Ammann back cla. **Still Pictures:** Michael Gunther front bl. **Tony Stone Images:** Renee Lynn front c.